GO
UNTOLD
TALES

6/4/79

Tek —
   Thanks for creating a warm and
wonderful space for me around your
fire. Thanks for everything in you
which is good and finds expression
in the paradoxes of your life ... for
laughter, tears and little fears,
for hospitality that knows no bounds,
for warmth and care and graying hair....
   Thank you, Lord, for Tek!
               much love,

Michael E. Moynahan, SJ

Moyna

P.S. Congratulations and blessings in your
continued and deepened ministry!

ISBN 0-89390-009-5
Library of Congress Catalog Card Number 79-64823

Acknowledgements:
    Cover design and layout: George F. Collopy
    Typography: Maureen Stuart

Published by Resource Publications, PO Box 444, Saratoga, CA 95070.

GOD OF UNTOLD TALES

Michael E. Moynahan, SJ

Published by Resource Publications,
PO Box 444, Saratoga, CA 95070.

Preface

The passageway to the heart's inner depths is like those ancient passages ingeniously contrived to thwart access to the tombs of Pharoahs and the treasures buried there. Apparent entrances deceptively leading nowhere; false turnings; traps to hurt the unwary and guard against final entry into the tomb. How cleverly, if mindlessly, each of us constructs the maze that guards against entrance into the heart's inner-most chambers!

In this collection of prayers, poems, and songs Michael Moynahan successfully negotiates the maze: he finds his way into our hearts. Quite simply, in speaking from his own inner depths he touches the heart of his reader; in pondering his own pilgrimage he speaks to the pilgrim in each of us. He holds up a mirror in which his reader can recognize a very similar self. He charts regions of the heart all too seldom explored, and even less seldom explored with such sensitivity, imagination, and wit. Not for nothing is his last name Moynahan!

Too often our very images of God—if I may borrow from the Pharoahs once again—mummify the Deity. We swathe God in bindings of our own making, not His. Hoping to preserve, we succeed only in making Him all but unrecognizable. The beguiling, refreshingly original imagery in this book invites the reader to think about God—and oneself—in new, more vital ways.

Reading the prayers in this book is something like being allowed to listen in on intimate conversations between two friends, one of whom just happens to be God. Prayer is as varied as the moods out of which we pray. The reader will encounter a rich variety here. Now gently taking God to task, now praising; songs of joy and appreciation, sad admissions of failure; questioning, telling, asking, giving. All of which makes me think that the Old Testament could have used an Irish psalmist! Happily for us, this book goes a long way toward making good the lack.

In his introduction Michael Moynahan says, "Hearing another's story can prompt us to believe in and share our own. It is, after all, us. And this is the only gift we have to give one another." In the name of all who know doubt in the midst of life's bewildering mystery, all who search and find only to search again, all who know hunger and thirst of soul—in the name of all of us fellow-pilgrims I thank Michael Moynahan for the gift he has shared in this delightful book.

Leo P. Rock, SJ
Santa Clara University
August 24, 1976

Introduction

What is man? If I asked you to describe him in one word, I think you would be hard pressed to find the one that satisfied you. Writers and artists have tried for centuries to capture man in prose, on canvas, in wood or metered verse. He has been described as a hero and a villain, a saint and a sinner, a liberator, an oppressor, thoughtful and thoughtless, careful and careless, adulterous, faithful, inspiring, despicable, virtuous, vicious, elated, despondent, a creature of moderation prone to extremes. So what is our picture of man but a montage of contradictory images. Is man good or evil? The answer is yes, for he is capable of both.

Of all the attempts to describe man, the one image that appeals most to me is that of the pilgrim. We are people who are constantly "on the way." We are searching for the identity of ourselves and others, and ultimately of God. And during our journey we must stop, at times, and rest. Since we travel together, we fill these brief respites re-creatively. We gather in the evening by the road. Huddled around a warm fire we pass the time sharing stories—tales of how we have discovered ourselves, our God and others on this pilgrimage. The journey never ends. The story is never finished.

Hearing another's story can prompt us to believe in and share our own. It is, after all, us. And this is the only gift we have to give one another. Carl Rogers once said that paradoxically it is when we share what is most personal to us that we can touch another in the very special depths of their own experience. It is in that spirit and with that hope that I presume to share these prayers, poems and songs with you. They are tales that depict the search and struggle of three years. They capture, in part, the discoveries I made of myself and others that inevitably led me to discover new dimensions of God. If they touch your experience; if they free you in any way to share your story; then they have been worth the telling.

I am forever grateful to those who have shared this pilgrimage with me. These tales are a reflection of our shared lives. To Leo, Wilkie, Bob, Jack, Steve and Bill; to each of the Jesuit Novices in Santa Barbara who made these years so full; to Bill Fulco who taught my spirit to dance; to my uncle, Richard O'Shaughnessy, who taught it to sing; and to John Mossi who has called it forth to play; to all of you I gratefully dedicate this book.

God grant you all happiness and length of days as we continue to share our journey, our stories, and our lives together.

Michael E. Moynahan, SJ
College of the Queen of Peace
March 25, 1976

Contents

God Of Untold Tales

O God who's found
in untold tales,
come catch us
walking on the road
away from all
that could have been.

Shake disappointment's
strangle hold
off our bruised
and heavy hearts.
Re-fresh and mind us.
Rekindle shattered dreams.
Take up the old
unfinished theme.

Let dread-full
melancholy scales
fall from our eyes
so we can see you
present in reality.

Help us find
your tell-tale care
here and now,
in simple things:
waiting, walking,
listening, talking,
healing.
Together
sharing all we have
and are,
broken bread,
companionship,
as we travel on
from old Jerusalems.

Today

Lord,
I stand before the door
of another day.
Behind me lay the piled-high ruins
of yesterday:
the worn out "if only's"
and the shattered "could have been's."
For the little good I did,
for the little I saw
and all I cannot see—thanks!
Fill me this morning with your Spirit.
Breathe into me your quickening exhilations.
Recreate me!
Awaken in me hope
and dreams of what can be.
Help me feel your touch
and let me know you are near.
Look into my heaped-up heart
and free an ounce of the love
I desperately hope is there.
I am your reflection.
Don't tire of being my mirror.
Continue revealing to me
the goodness of mine
and every person's heart—
for my vision is faulty,
and my memory is short.
And finally, Lord,
help me give away some more
of all you give to me.
And when I've given all I think I have away,
work your water-into-wine wonder
in me again.
Renew me and fill me up
to give away some more!

Thanksgiving

Lord,
I thank you for another day
and all the hope it brings.
I thank you for the morning sun
whose light illumines darkest night.
For mysteries that the sun reveals:
for dew-glistening grass
and speckled-white waves,
for pines that bend
and play wind's tune,
for oaks that seem to stand unmoved,
for frail-winged birds
who brave the gusts
that always stand
between themselves and destination,
for scampering little furry squirrels
that choose to miss a meal
instead of choking
on a winter day,
for all that is, that lives and breathes,
I give you thanks.

You have gifted me in many ways,
you faithful, loving, goodly God,
for this, I give you thanks.
For thoughts that flash across my mind;
for songs that dance inside my head;
for feelings locked in heavy hearts;
for hands that hold unsteady pens;
for eyes that see
through mud-caked goodness;
for timid mouths that bluster,
bumble, mumble reassuring words;
for less than steady lips
that break a winter's frost
with warm caress;
for searching, struggling, bungling fingers
that break through prison bars
and slowly open unlocked doors;

for all that is the mystery
of myself and all the others:
brothers, sisters...
I give you thanks.

May this moment of light linger
longer, stronger,
some far off day when vision dims,
and light my personal darkness.

Good God, I believe you are just that,
maybe more, but certainly
no less.
Touch and heal in all of us
that which finds it hard to believe.

Weekday Revelation

My mind recalls the time
we two first met.
You had come to talk, to question.
You had ascended a make-believe mountain
seeking wisdom, the meaning of life,
and directions on how to plod
down other cosmic avenues.
You were troubled, frightened, worried,
exhilerated in a melancholic way.
You were happy and sad
all rolled into one.
Tears were in your eyes.
Love was caught somewhere
between your heart and throat.
You were searching and struggling.
I felt helpless.
You wanted answers
and I could only smile
and reassure you with my doubts.
You thought I was strong
but couldn't see me
wrestling with my weakness.
You held out open hands for help.
You opened wide your child-full heart.
I wanted desperately to give you
all you sought,
but knew my all
was much too little.

We sat and talked and cried and laughed.
We shared and cared and listened
to each other's words,
and what our words could never say.
And through it all that night,
through the tears and the love,
the laughter, doubt and asking,
one solitary thing I thought
with clarity astounding even me—
here is Christ:

hungry, poor, naked, in prison and alone.
You there in chains and pauper's clothes
called forth the priest in me.
You touched and freed the Christ in me
to serve the Christ in you.
For a fleeting weekday revelation—
I give you thanks, O Lord.

Faces

When I look into their faces, Lord,
and see your light:
sparkling, working there,
reborn again, alive;
when I look into their eyes
and see your life:
the goodness, beauty,
wrestled-with beliefs
and time-worn hopes;
when their wrinkled brows
and mustered smiles,
their sun-burnt trusting hands
reveal their clay-kept treasure:
loving, aching, yearning hearts;
in all of this
I see what blood shot eyes
are often blinded to:
You.

You are present, Lord,
working there in each of them
and sneaking out in constant
unexpected revelations.
Never the right time.
Never the right place.
Never the looked for way.
And so, you all too often
escape our fragile, frazzled,
easily distracted gaze.

Come, then, you who know us
better than we know ourselves.
Do not let your love
escape our notice.
Heal us of our blindness.

Wrench from our clutching hands
all the idols we have made
and fearfully,
tearfully cling to:

all those things that promise life
but only deal out death.

We call to you in anger, disillusion,
disappointment and confusion.
We lift our tight clenched fists
and beg you come, heal,
gift us with your presence
and your love.

Send us the warming
power of your Spirit.
Melt our grasping,
needy, greedy grips.
Open our hands
and minds and hearts
to the ways you do
come to us, heal us,
love us and gift us.

Simple Things

Simple things:
all that goes unnoticed,
so easily overlooked;
all that does not shout or squeak,
forgotten things brushed aside,
bordering almost on being lost—
the ways you come to us.

Interruptions:
the constant barging in—
from only God knows where—
the comings, goings,
always calling unannounced,
defying the collar starch
of prayer-full protocol,
avoiding with
unyielding resolution
systems, schedules and schools—
all those neat and tidy
transcendental rendezvous.

Longings:
the gnawing, clawing,
constant hunger deep within
which pushes me
in panicked search
to grasp and gorge myself
on what can never satisfy;
the numbing, aching,
anguished urge to
unconditionally declare
my inner emptiness
and open up
to overdue and needed healing.

Waitings:
the silent,
sweat-filled watching,
finger biting questioning

and fearful wondering.
Who will come?
What will happen?
Legs that ran so swiftly,
freeze.
Paralysis.
An end to fleeing.
The freeing,
doubt-filled pause that refreshes.
Always anxious, never knowing,
wondering if Egypt was not
better than this senseless,
endless wandering
and heavy hearted waiting
in the desert.

Lord,
I believe.
Help all that in me
that finds it hard
to wait,
to long,
to let you constantly
break into my life.

The God Pursuing Us

Where shall I look
for you today,
you teasing, pleasing God?

My mind begins
to shake off sleep
and cautiously anticipate
what comic plots and schemes
this new day holds.

What favorite place?
What worn-out time?
What always unexpected way
will freeing, fleeing
playful God
bump into fearful man?

You God of Games
that never lets us rest
or set down rules
of cold predictability.
What fools we are
at times like this!

We jump and run,
we scratch and claw.
Exhilarating joy seems lost
in our adult intensity.
We struggle constantly to find
a God who runs too fast.

If only we could stop,
step back and see
the humor of this game.
Just stop and linger,
looking long and hard
at what surrounds us.

Ah! The pause that refreshes.
For in that moment's rest

there, we could meet
the God pursuing us.

Come and seek and find us, Lord.
Run after us
until we have to stop for breath.
Then quickly tag us,
touch us, free us—
let us know that we are found.

Lord Of Days Gone By

O God,
who long ago I knew,
who walked with me
and made me laugh
at my pretentious sanctity:
you seem an out-of-focus myth,
a story told so long ago
that memory cannot collect
the old dismembered ashes
of a youthful, warm
relationship.

Where are you now,
O Lord of days gone by?

The thousand ways
that we could kiss
and touch: our minds and hearts,
our wills and memories.
The thousand ways
that came with love
and always flowed so naturally
now seem contrived
or filled with my hypocrisy.
Tainted.
Painted charcoal gray
and filed away
with all the painful
best forgotten things.

Pretending
will not make
the ugly questions
go away.

Why have I squandered
and abused
the love first offered me?
Why do I twist

and wrestle free
each time your healing touch
approaches me?
Why do I constantly
run off and hide
from awe-full
understanding eyes?

You know what I'm
afraid to own:
the deep desire
of my tired heart
to here and now
be found by you.

Come melt me,
God whose fire
once warmed my soul.
Free me from the lonely
dead-wood weight
that slowly smothers
this unfaithful lover's
battered, tattered,
once upon a time
real feeling heart.

The Unexpected Guest

Why is it, Lord,
you wake us,
shake us up
with constant
unpredictability?

Is it asking you
too much to humor—
even pamper—
those of us who wait
for you to visit
with some calculated
regularity?

Do you take
undue delight
in catching people
off their guard?
Must we be
so under-dressed
and ill-disposed
to meet you
as you strangle us
with relative surprise?

You always find us
unprepared to welcome you
or let you in
our all too tightly
scheduled day
and much too crowded world.

Always the wrong time.
Always the wrong place.
Invariably you creep and crawl
or sneak into our lives
in some unexpected way.

But—
Your time

is all time.
It's now...
and then some.

Your place
is here.
It's any place
and everywhere I stand
or chance to meet another.

Your way
is always.
Slowly filling
each unpretentious moment
with wondrous possibility.

O Lord,
whose presence frees
the child in us
to be wonder-full,
break into our chilled
arthritic lives.
Surprise us all.
Don't warn us.
Warm us!
Strengthen and renew
our twisted hopes
and crippled hearts.
Somehow with unbounded Spirit
help us meet you
where you are,
where we are,
always here in the
constantly emerging,
the once-in-a-life-time
Now.

God Who's Hidden Deep Within

(I)
O God,
who's hidden
deep within the faces,
places, scattered thoughts,
the strong and contradictory things
that complicate and just confuse
the feelings of an aging heart,
draw near here now
and counsel me.

(II)
So many times
I've longed and prayed
or looked for ways
of wading deeper
into simple mystery.
An often lonely,
hungry friend
looks for closer company.
And in this search—
polarities:
equal parts of
thirst for truth
and actual dishonesty.

(III)
What does it mean
to follow you?
Must I embark
with neck-break speed,
rushing on collision's course
and meet with sure catastrophe
on Jerusalem's old road?

(IV)
To love you
is no easy task.
It costs

(but who keeps count?)
too much at times.
Why must I constantly
court death
and watch so many
golden thoughts and
sterling silver feelings
all go up in smoke?

Love means that I must
wander through the rubble
of my squandered dreams
and in the fragile ashes
of painful burnt-out memories
find the tiny seeds
of new beginnings.

(V)
Following you
sight often fails
as I struggle hard
for some small trace
of where you wandered most.
The closer I get
the more I feel my stomach
turning somersaults.
A cluttered head
questions my ability
to imitate the Master plan.

To follow is to serve:
in season, out of season,
not only all the pretty ones
who frequent my Romantic world—
no, that is my way—
but everyone.

Your way saw you
waste your time
with uglies in the market place.
Because you were so prodigal
you helped to heal

our broken world
and fractured personalities.
You made us uglies
beautiful beyond belief.
Lord I believe,
but help my little faith!

(VI)
God of my every thought,
Lord of my heart's desire,
in my search for you
I ask three things:
give my knowledge clarity;
give my love intensity;
and let my journey
follow in your footsteps
so that my service
can be patterned
after yours.

Swift-footed Lord

O Lord,
my body's beat numb
from forced escape:
those aimless, hurt-full,
desert-driven wanderings
that I compose for distance
and execute myself.
I am too tired
to carry on the race,
that never ending chase
as You, my swift-footed Lord,
try hard to capture me.

But still I run
and waste the very breath
that's life.
As if possessed I press on,
dashing mad;
sad and fitfull starting;
stopping briefly, rushing on,
off again and driven
by the haunting fear of what?
Of what the mind
could never guess,
and only heart would know.

O God, who chases after me,
driven hard by love
that knows no bounds,
continue now to follow fast
as your confused and desperate friend
struggles to elude
your gentle glance.
Advance, surround,
confound me with a lover's
irrepressible tenacity.
And let this weary runner
once again: be touched,
be healed, be found.

Prestidigitating God

O prestidigitating God,
you captivate the child in us
with wide-eyed wonder.
Hearts thump, jaws drop,
hand-covered mouths gasp,
bodies bump jumping
with tip-toed excitement
at your fantastical array,
endless display of illusions.

Are your wonders
simply slight of hand?
Magic boggles, blocks our mind.
Are there explanations
only hearts can comprehend?

We see a paschal pattern,
the woof and warp
of all your tricks repeated,
(for in the ecology of salvation
these things are recycled)
worked a hundred thousand times
in nature's circus,
the arena of life that surrounds us.

We come upon you in mid-act.
Where moments before nothing stood,
suddenly, POOF! something's there.
But from where?
You calmly snatch victory
from the snarling, snapping, jagged jaws
of every day defeat.
Next you find unexpected faith
in the empty hat of doubt.

You continue to amaze us
by pulling hope—that rabbit's foot—
from the time-worn,
torn sleeve of life's despair.

And finally, for your grand finale,
you quickly build
with drum roll and trumpet fanfare
to your last and greatest trick,
the prank unparalleled,
pulled on all of us,
that wonderful catastrophe:
life from death.

O God of constant paradox,
you disconcert us with your ways.
Continue now to draw us
deeper into mystery.
Confound our inquisitions,
steel our timid hearts
with the wonder of a great
Magician's love.

God Who Goes Unrecognized

O God
who goes unrecognized
despite our seasoned endeavoring,
once again we wait and watch
and hope with expectation's
brim-filled stockings.
Shocking?

We muster all that's left
of our precious little energy:
struggling, searching,
snatching, spending
who we are and what we have
reluctantly—
a last gasp grasp
for an ounce of Christmas joy.

And for what?
Do you simply toy with us?
We wait for someone
who has come.
We frantically prepare
our selves and homes
for a guest already arrived.
He has been living, breathing,
feeling, longing
in the hearts and hopes of all
who smell to highest heaven.
He is regrettably overlooked,
hardly noticed
out of season.

O God of anonymity,
break through waxed ears
and frozen stares.
Release the hope, the healing,
the longed for
pause that refreshes—
peace on earth.

Fill us full of overdue
good will towards all who dwell
with us on earth.
"The spirit of Christmas past, present and to
come"

God Of Laughter

O God of laughter,
Lord of clowns,
whose presence
we have often found
can rescue us
when we are buried deep
beneath the stern drawn
mask of tragedy,
deliver us now
and at the hour of our
melancholic propensities.

We vacillate
with expertise
between two contradictory poles:
dread-full, weighted
somberness,
and comic spontaneity.
Like veterans
of too many wars
we settle down uneasily
to what some label normalcy.
Do not give us this day
our seasoned schizophrenia.

We share your likeness
godly prankster.
You bless us each
with humor's gift:
salvific madness,
therepeutic insanity.
Help us reclaim it
for our homes.
Do not lead us
into the temptation
of oppressively distorting
all we call reality.

God of jesters,

care-fool Lord,
touch us now
with your healing power:
the gentle breeze
of laughter's breath.
And in return
accept from us
all those tears
that never fall
but pass through heart's
redemptive fire
and rise
higher,
bubble-up and out
into comic sounds,
knowing smiles,
renewed belief
and bolstered hope,
the promise
of another day.

Lord Of When And Where And How

O God,
whose presence I have found
in constant interruptions
that confound an otherwise
well-ordered day,
why do you pursue us
in such annoying ways?

Your unpredictibility
unsettles well-constructed worlds.
You seem to take undue delight
in throwing off our schedule.

A clever master of disguise,
you push and shove relentlessly
intruding with no "Pardon me!"
into what we call "reality."
You masquerade in countless ways
as the greedy, needy
all around us.

Why continue to come
so unannounced,
and expect us to meet you
here and now?
Especially when we much prefer
to plan things out
or give our all
in one fell swoop—
the once-a-year
"united way."

O Lord of when
and where and how,
continue now and then again
to stretch us past
the breaking point.
Help us make
the time and space
so you can sneak

and pry your way
past Apollo's sentinel
into our tightly
scheduled day.
Drop in unexpectedly
in hunger, fear,
in laughter, tears,
in loneliness
and a thousand cries for help
that hound us,
surround us,
everyday.

O God Who Slowly Comes To Be

O God,
who slowly comes to be
in all I think
or feel and do,
at times I find it
hard to wait,
to hope when all
seems lost or gone.

You stretch my little
faith, at times.
For when I've sown
a seed or two,
immediately I start to strain.
I scrutinize the fallow ground
and search for shoots,
some speck of life.
Too soon I flirt
with old despair:
a novice planter's petulance,
showing signs of nervousness,
tapping fingers, anxious feet,
as if this ritual restlessness
could speed things up
or get the looked for
quick results.

You certainly must laugh somewhere.
Why do you tease me
in this way?
Why do you let me herniate
as I struggle hard to see
the very thing I'm blinded to?
You seem to lead me
into play.
There I catch, however brief,
a tantilizing glimpse
of you.

So I march on

with hope renewed.
Somewhat less reluctantly
I now pursue you
caught up in this
endless game
of self-disclosing
hide and seek.

O Lord,
for whom I hunger, thirst,
you know the longings
of my soul.
You alone can find your way
past disillusion's tattered dreams
to what I hope for,
need and want,
all I seek impatiently.
Take my trembling,
tear-filled hands.
Embrace my timid,
fearful heart.
Be my companion
as I wait in faith
for my looked for
Lord to come.

O God Who Loves To Be Found Out

O God
who loves
to be found out,
we thank you
for the tell-tale signs:
the thousand hints,
clues left behind
that slowly lead us
on to
you.

The search
is often burdensome,
more complicated
than need be
because of our ineptitude.
We struggle onward
comically,
tripping over evidence
(the constant X
that marks the spot),
resembling in this
sleuth-charade
a bumbling Watson or Clousseau
more than a clever-witted Holmes.

O Lord who's veiled delightfully
in episodic mystery,
come catch our curiosity
and lead us on
a lightsome chase.
Yield a flashing glimpse,
some tiny revelation
of the one pursued.
Tantalize us
with this prize.

Gives us eyes
to carry on
and search for what

we dimly see:
what numbed heads
must ever onward guess at—
our heart's guest—
identity.

God Of Gentle Whisperings

O God of gentle whisperings,
your voice is heard
in simple things
which crowded in my busy world
go unattended, overlooked.

Perhaps I take undue delight,
part of my romantic whim,
to search for you on mountain tops,
in seismographic happenings
and Cecile B. De Millish things.

I look for you in thunder, Lord,
the pounding, drowning sounds
of pretentious majesty.
Longing to be overwhelmed
and captured by a trumphet blast
I quickly learn, saddened some,
you are not there.

Ready almost to turn away,
my strength, defenses all but drained,
you come to me in gentle rain
and quicken my worn parched roots.
An easily forgotten breeze
renews the hope that almost died
and once again I know you're near.

O God, who tries to speak to me,
your softly uttered murmurings
can breathe new life
into a faint and wounded heart.
Come here, then, now
and shake it with your Word.
Shape it! Save it too!
Be healing food, be life and hope
for a hungry, lost
and struggling soul.

Poverty

Because I do not
want to cling,
or in my silly
childish ways
to clutch or hide
or hoard anything;

Because I do not
want to hold
to what is easy
and safe to do,
all that's old,
all that I knew;

Because I want
to empty out
all the things
I claim to need,
that only keep me
out of reach
from what could really
satisfy
the aching-longing
hunger-thirst
I often feel
within my heart;

I want to throw
my frightened self
into my God's
embracing—
faithful hands.

And what will come
of this?
Perhaps I'll meet
my Lord in poverty,
and stripped of
many useless things
there will be room

for him to fill
me now
full of his love.
And this, I know,
is all I need.

Chastity

Because I want
to love not one
or two
or few
but many;

Because I want
to touch them all
with mind and heart
and all I am;

Because I feel
so much inside,
too much to give
to just one other;
I want to try
before my God
to live a life
of constant love
that will, of course,
have ups and downs,
but hopefully
will be the way
that I'm set free
with stumbling,
fumbling,
all too weak
and fail-prone Peter
to try again
and love some more.

Obedience

Because I know
I only see
a tiny part—
so little of all
we call reality;

Because my body
cannot take
this shoulder drooping,
stooping load,
the heavy day-in
day-out cares
of a goodly God
who's always there;

Because my vision
often fails
and misses
all the intricacies
of past, present
and future possibilities;

I wish to give
my Lord a chance
to plot the course
of an ever-new
unfolding life,
and play the role
that he knows best:
God of my destiny.

Michael E. Moynahan, SJ is currently pursuing doctoral studies in Liturgy and Drama at the Graduate Theological Union. A native of Phoenix, Arizona, he entered the Society of Jesus in 1962. From 1970 to 1973 he pursued a Master of Divinity degree at the Jesuit School of Theology in Berkeley, California. Ordained in 1973, Father Moynahan served as assistant Director of Novices from 1973 to 1976 for the California Providence. He has been a regular contributor to *Modern Liturgy* and also contributed to *Liturgy* and *Momentum*.